TRIGGER

TRIGGER

Daniel MacIvor

Trigger
first published 2012 by
Scirocco Drama
An imprint of J. Gordon Shillingford Publishing Inc.

Scirocco Drama Editor: Glenda MacFarlane
Cover photo of Molly Parker and Tracy Wright by Guntar Kravis
Cover design by Terry Gallagher/Doowah Design Inc.
Author photo by Guntar Kravis
Printed and bound in Canada on 100% post-consumer recycled paper.

We acknowledge the financial support of the Manitoba Arts Council and The Canada Council for the Arts for our publishing program.

Library and Archives Canada Cataloguing in Publication

MacIvor, Daniel, 1962-
Trigger/Daniel MacIvor.

A screenplay.
ISBN 978-1-897289-80-8

I. Title.

PS8575.I86T75 2012 C812'.54 C2012-905332-5

J. Gordon Shillingford Publishing
P.O. Box 86, RPO Corydon Avenue, Winnipeg, MB Canada R3M 3S3

Production Information

Trigger premiered in 2010, with the following cast and crew:

VIC .... Tracy Wright

KAT .... Molly Parker

HOST .... Daniel MacIvor

WAITER #2 .... Bob Martin

ROCKER CHICK #1 .... Melinda Shankar

ROCKER CHICK #3 .... Aislinn Paul

CRAZY GIRL .... Mallary Davenport

HILLARY .... Sarah Polley

BEEBEE .... Lenore Zann

HONEY .... Adam Barrett

WAITER #1 .... Greg Calderone

BRIAN .... Don McKellar

ROCKER CHICK #2 .... Marline Yan

ROCKER CHICK .... Samantha Munro

BILLY .... Callum Keith Rennie

CABBIE .... Alan Zweig

BUCKY .... Julian Richings

Directed by Bruce McDonald

Executive Producers: Dany Chiasson, Hugh Dillon, Bryan Gliserman, Sarah Haywood, Callum Keith Rennie

Producers: Leonard Farlinger, Jennifer Jonas

Daniel MacIvor

Daniel MacIvor was born in Cape Breton, Nova Scotia. He is the author and director of numerous award-winning theatre productions including *See Bob Run, Wild Abandon, 2-2-Tango, This Is A Play, The Soldier Dreams, You Are Here, How It Works, A Beautiful View, Communion,* and *Bingo!* From 1987 to 2007 with Sherrie Johnson he ran da da kamera, a respected international touring company that brought his work to Australia, the U.K. and toured extensively throughout the US and Canada. With long time collaborator Daniel Brooks, he created the solo performances *House, Here Lies Henry, Monster, Cul-de-sac* and *This Is What Happens Next*. Daniel won a GLAAD Award and a *Village Voice* Obie Award in 2002 for his play *In On It,* which was presented at PS 122 in New York. In 2006, Daniel received the Governor General's Literary Award for Drama for his collection of plays *I Still Love You*. In 2008, he was awarded the prestigious Siminovitch Priize in Theatre.

Foreword

My letter to Daniel asked if he would consider writing a movie inspired by an unholy pairing of *My Dinner with Andre* and *Hard Core Logo*. I had long beern a fan and admirer of Daniel's writing, his performances and his plays; especially his one-man shows *Monster, House* and *Here Lies Henry*. Some of the best theatre I've ever seen.

Daniel, the hardest working man in showbiz, said yes.

His instructions were to write a two-hander for Calllum Keith Rennie and Hugh Dillon (two of my favourite actors), in which the guys would reprise their roles as Billy Tallent and Joe Dick from our '95 movie *Hard Core Logo*. Great.

Daniel said, "OK, so what's it about?"

"Dunno," I said. "Old friends getting back together? Healing old wounds. Reconnecting."

"Uh huh," said Daniel. "Let me see what I can do."

In very short order—perhaps it was weeks, maybe a month—Daniel came over with the first draft.

"I hope you don't mind," Daniel began tentatively, "but I took some liberties with the 'what is this about'." OK.

It's structured around the Twelve Step Program."

I read it. Loved it. Smart. Emotional. True. Funny. Very much our Hard Core characters 15 years on from when we last met them.

Daniel and I loved it and we thought Callum and Hugh would too, but after a read through and a midnight call to me—it was clear the boys weren's loving it. As much as they loved Daniel, the writing and the story, they were not buying the whole AA Twelve Step thing.

That was kind of a big problem. I had commissioned the script for my favourite actors, from my favourite writer.

What to do?

Rewrite? Get another writer?

I called Daniel and levelled with him and,as was quite possibly the end of of the project, re remarkably unfreaked out.

"Hmm," he said. "OK, so if we want to keep the script we won't get Hugh and Callum. So do we keep the script? You tell me."

"Yes," I said.

OK, but now what do we do about our actors?

Maybe we cast 10 year-olds as Joe Dick and Billy Tallent.

Maybe we make them chicks.

Hey.

Interesting.

Tracy Wright?

Molly Parker?

Sold.

With fewer changes than you imagine, Daniel presented the "polished" version of the screenplay and it was great, even more exciting to have our rock 'n rollers female and created for our two favourite actresses—Tracy and Molly.

We asked them and thankfully, they said yes.

However, as I went about trying to raise money for the shoot, something happened that changes everthing: Tracy was diagnosed with pancreatic cancer and given only months to live.

Our whole community was devestated by the news. We grew up with Tracy Wright in theatre, film and TV. We came of age with Tracy Wright. Tracy was simply the greatest. The best. She always set the bar for what was cool and what was amazing. We were in shock.

Don McKellar, Tracy's long-time partner in love and crime, married her in the new year in a stunningly romantic and perfest ceremony and party. Whispered at that very party was the question, "What about Tracy's movie?" Maybe work would keep her alive or at least focus all our attention away from something none of us wanted to think about.

Out of those whispers stepped up two remarkable producers—Jennifer Jonas and Leonard Farlinger. Within weeks they brought the film community in Toronto together and suddenly we were shooting. Callum Rennie became a very generous investor in the film and made a cameo appearance. Hugh Dillon invested. Producers, film companies, and unions stepped up and helped make our miracle project happen, while Tracy and Molly made magic out of Daniel's script.

Tracy died shortly after the movie was shot, but lives gloriously in this movie. Thank you Tracy.

Thank you Molly Parker for being the wondrous friend and actress you are.

And thank you Daniel MacIvor for your fierce truth and beauty.

Readers, enjoy.

Bruce McDonald
Visual Mechanic
Commander of the Northern Tribes
Autumn 2012

1 INT. SHEPHERD'S BUSH EMPIRE - NIGHT - 1995

Black and white 16mm footage of a band on stage at the famous Empire Club in London's Shepherd's Bush. We do not hear the sound of the footage but rather we hear a sound track of DELICATE MODERNIST STRINGS. Two young and rather fucked up young women, VIC and KAT, front the band. VIC is all dark and fuck-you Patti Smith, on vocals and lead guitar. KAT is smouldering, staggering supermodel glamour on bass. An anonymous DRUMMER and KEYBOARD PLAYER round out the combo. A TITLE appears on screen: "Trigger". The footage jump cuts through the gig. The women seem more involved with pissing one another off than engaging with the audience. VIC taunts KAT while KAT ignores VIC. At one point VIC approaches KAT and aggressively grabs her head and licks her face. A second title appears on screen: "Empire Shepherd's Bush, 1995". A jump cut to KAT standing at the front of the stage, she is no longer playing her bass and seems to be flirting with someone in the crowd. VIC approaches KAT and gives her a mild bodycheck, KAT staggers. A jump cut to KAT yanking on VIC's hair. A jump cut to the two women no longer playing but seemingly in the midst of a verbal shouting match. VIC throws down her guitar, stomps it and storms off stage. KAT turns to the audience and cheers raising her arms. After a moment KAT seems a bit lost, she looks around as if not sure where she is. She staggers a moment then passes out cold. A title appears: "The final gig". Fade to black, Music continues.

2 INT. CANOE RESTAURANT - DAY - TORONTO - PRESENT

Upscale, haute-minimalist restaurant high in the Toronto sky. All sleek lines and open space. The sound track of delicate modernist strings continues. VIC sits at a table waiting, she is older but still dresses the part of the rebel-rocker. A HOST approaches the table.

HOST: A drink while you're waiting Ma'am?

VIC: I'm fine for now.

The HOST departs. VIC looks at her watch, takes out reading glasses and a book. She begins to read.

3 INT. BOUTIQUE HOTEL / WORKOUT ROOM - DAY

Close on KAT's face, running, sweating.

She is also older but has spent a good deal of time and money keeping up her youth.

There is a sense of urgency about her as she continues to sweat, her breathing heavy, it is as if she is running for her life. After a few moments we hear a digital beeping.

KAT slows down. She has been running on a treadmill in an upscale hotel spa/gym. KAT's body is fit, healthy and she wears slick workout gear. She answers her Blackberry.

KAT: Yeah?

4 INT. CANOE RESTAURANT - DAY

VIC sits holding the book in front of her staring out a window at the impressive view of Toronto. We see the book's title: "The Spirituality of Imperfection." A WAITER approaches.

WAITER 1: Have you had a chance to look at our wine list Ma'am?

VIC: No—I mean yeah—no thanks.

WAITER 1: Sure. A drink while you wait Ma'am?

VIC: I'm good right now.

WAITER 1: Certainly Ma'am.

WAITER 1 departs. VIC watches daggers after WAITER 1. VIC calms herself and goes back to her book. She looks at her watch.

5 EXT. BOUTIQUE HOTEL / ROOM - DAY

A spacious and elegant room. KAT rushes to leave. She looks at the time, she is late.

6 INT. BOUTIQUE HOTEL / LOBBY - DAY

KAT rushes through the elegant lobby and out into a waiting town car while talking on her Blackberry. Though bundled up against the cold she still manages to look effortlessly chic.

7 INT. CANOE RESTAURANT - DAY

VIC furrows her brow over a passage in the book. She puts the book down to think a moment. She looks at an orchid in a small vase which decorates the table. She touches it gently. She is distracted by the delicate ambient music. She doesn't like it. She looks around the room at the other diners. Corporate TROPHY WIVES getting drunk on day-glo martinis, a gaggle of YOUNG BUSINESSMEN basking in a post-deal-closing glow pounding back the imported beer. She doesn't like any of them. She looks at the frayed cuff on her jacket. WAITER 2 appears.

WAITER 2: You won't be having wine Ma'am?

VIC: No.

WAITER 2: Shall I leave the wine list for your friend?

VIC: How do you know it's a friend? Maybe it's a mortal enemy. Maybe we're going to do muskets at twenty paces right here in the restaurant.

WAITER 2: Sorry Ma'am.

VIC: And could people stop calling me "Ma'am"?

WAITER 2: Sure. A drink?

VIC: No! Do you people not communicate? No I don't want a drink. I don't want a fuzzy navel or a Tom Collins or a bottle of Jack Daniels with a dirty glass or a bottle of wine that costs as much as a well for an African village. No.

WAITER 2: Sure. OK. Sorry.

WAITER 2 sheepishly departs. VIC immediately regrets having lost her cool.

8 INT. CANOE RESTAURANT / WAITER'S STATION - DAY

VIC comes up behind WAITER 2.

VIC: Hey listen. I'm sorry about losing it there. I don't like waiting and I'm waiting and you know, I shouldn't have taken it out on you. Just something I'm, you know, working on.

WAITER 2: No problem.

VIC: Great. And you can bring me a club soda?

WAITER 2: *(Rather fearfully.)* We only serve San Pellegrino.

VIC: Right. Tap water's good. Thanks.

VIC departs. As she walks back to her table she passes a woman at a table alone, her menu in front of her face. As VIC passes the woman drops her menu and watches after VIC. The woman is SICK VIC, this is VIC but a version of VIC as she would be today had she not made more positive choices in her life. SICK VIC has a grey pallor, yellow teeth and the devil in her eyes. SICK VIC watches after VIC, grins and goes back to her menu.

9 INT. TELEVISION STUDIO / EDITING ROOM - DAY

KAT and an EDITOR watch a monitor. KAT gives the editor some quick notes before leaving him to tinker with the scene. As she leaves she answers a call on her Blackberry.

10 INT. CANOE RESTAURANT - DAY

VIC is at the very edge of her patience. She has finished her tap water and looks at her watch.

Suddenly a voice nearby.

SICK VIC: Can I get you a beverage Ma'am?

VIC looks up angry. It is SICK VIC standing at the table. She grins down at VIC.

VIC: Fuck you.

SICK VIC: *(Grinning.)* Maybe later.

SICK VIC departs. VIC bows her head and breathes.

11 INT. CANOE RESTAURANT - DAY

A moment later. At the entrance of the dining room KAT looks into the restaurant. She sees VIC, she feels trepidation, she thinks twice and then glides into the restaurant.

At the table VIC takes one more look at her watch and prepares to leave.

KAT: I'm so sorry.

KAT arrives at the table all apologies but a cool mask of calm. VIC settles back in, working hard not to be resentful. KAT's phone rings. KAT looks at the phone.

Oh shit. I've got to—

VIC: Uh huh.

KAT: *(On phone.)* Yeah?… The darker one… Because the show is sunny enough it doesn't need the sunny theme… It's too twee… Twee … Butterflies and rainbows… The darker one… It's not that dark. It's not a dirge. Good. Yes.

KAT hangs up and puts the phone on the table.

That's going on vibrate right now. I've been working as a music advisor for Lifetime in L.A., incidental stuff, themes. And they want to rebrand the Canadian version so I convinced them to send me here for a few days. I could have done the work online but this way I get the flight and the hotel paid for. You know how it goes.

VIC: Not really.

KAT: Anyway. I'm sorry I'm late I know you hate waiting. We said six thirty right?

VIC: Six o'clock.

KAT: Really. You've been waiting forty-five minutes?

VIC: I was early.

KAT: How early?

VIC: It doesn't matter— About fifteen minutes.

KAT: You waited an hour! Something's changed. Back in the day you wouldn't have waited an hour for anyone. Maybe for your dealer. Oh give me a hug.

KAT rises and moves to VIC. VIC rises. An odd hug. KAT looks at VIC.

You look terrific.

VIC: You look terrible.

KAT: *(Laughing.)* No I don't.

VIC: And I don't look terrific.

They sit.

KAT: How are you?

VIC: *(Sighs.)* Uh huh.

KAT: Oh right, you hate that question.

VIC: Some things have changed but I still hate that question.

KAT: Right.

VIC: Do you want me to ask how you are?

KAT: Only if you're interested.

A moment.

VIC: How are you?

KAT: Good. Busy. Tired. Hungry. You've had a look at the menu right?

VIC: I had a chance yeah.

KAT: Plus they'll do up something special I came here quite a bit last time I was in town and I got to know the chef. It's great to see you. You know I wouldn't have kept you waiting an hour. I just never thought you'd be early. I was thinking I was just fifteen minutes behind. I was sure it was six thirty, I wrote it down somewhere.

(Re: Blackberry) I try to write things down in here but I can't work technology. I keep pretending but I should just go back to a date book and a watch.

The network gave it to me and I was too embarrassed to ask for instructions. Back home I think I'm the only person in LA who still uses a land-line.

VIC: Home?

WAITER 2 appears.

WAITER 2: *(Rather tentatively to KAT.)* Can I get you a drink?

KAT: A drink? Well… *(To VIC.)* What do you think?

VIC: You're drinking?

KAT: You?

VIC: No. You?

KAT: No. But…

VIC: But?

KAT: No.

A moment.

(To WAITER 2.) San Pellegrino, big bottle, lime on the side—is the lime fresh?

WAITER 2: Oh yes.

KAT: Lime on the side, no ice. Thanks. *(To VIC.)* You ready to order?

VIC: Sure.

KAT: *(To WAITER 2.)* Is Henry in the kitchen today?

WAITER 2: Henry's not here anymore.

KAT: Oh no, where's Henry?

WAITER 2: He went to Ultra.

KAT: *(To VIC.)* Oh, we should have gone to Ultra.

WAITER 2: But Denise is here, she mentored with Henry.

KAT: Do you still do that quail?

WAITER 2: Yes.

KAT: Great, I'll have the quail, no starch, organic greens.

WAITER 2: Sure. *(Turning to VIC.)* And… You?

VIC: *(Pointing to menu.)* What's this?

WAITER 2: Potato soup, it's very delicious.

VIC: Just a salad.

WAITER 2: We have a selection—

VIC: The number one.

WAITER 2: OK.

WAITER 2 moves to depart.

VIC: *(Picking up flower vase from table and handing it to WAITER 2.)* We can do without this.

WAITER 2 leaves with the flower. After a moment.

KAT: This thing tonight.

VIC: How embarrassing.

KAT: Yeah I know.

VIC: "Women In Rock"? Why not Women in Labour? Will there be a bake sale too?

KAT: It's a tribute.

VIC: To who?

KAT: Well, to us for one.

VIC: Are they giving out medals? I'd rather have cash.

KAT: They want us to do something.

VIC: Uh huh.

KAT: They'd like us to do something. I mean I'm not prepared to do anything.

VIC: I'm not sure I'm going.

KAT: You have to go.

VIC: No I don't.

KAT: You have to at least go. I mean you don't have to do something.

VIC: I'm not doing anything.

KAT: But you have to go.

VIC: No I don't.

KAT: No true no, you don't have to. It would be nice though.

VIC: Nice for who?

KAT: OK fine. I mean it's happening and I'm here…

VIC: I thought you were here because you're working.

KAT: No, well yes, but I planned the work around tonight. I'm here for tonight.

VIC: That's nice.

KAT: I could have done this work at home.

VIC: Home?

KAT: Sorry?

VIC: L.A. is home now?

KAT: Well as much as L.A. can be.

VIC: You and L.A.

KAT: Sliver Lake is nice. Malibu. Overall it's not that different from here. Other than the weather, and that you can't walk anywhere.

VIC: I've read that.

KAT: You've spent time in LA.

VIC: In a hotel room.

KAT: You should come down.

VIC: Are you doing any modelling these days?

KAT: It wasn't modelling.

VIC: Well what would you call having your picture taken in a magazine to sell clothes?

KAT: It wasn't selling clothes.

VIC: Well you weren't wearing much clothing that's true.

KAT: It's ancient history.

A moment.

It was fun. What I remember of it. I was drunk most of the time.

WAITER 2 appears with water for KAT and VIC. KAT goes silent until WAITER 2 departs.

I can't believe you're still carrying that around.

VIC: I'm not carrying anything around.We're just "catching up".

A moment.

KAT: So what have you been up to?

VIC: Not much.

KAT: But you're good right? I'm hearing you're good.

VIC: Where are you hearing that?

KAT: From Bill.

VIC: That asshole.

KAT: He says you're in touch.

VIC: He still wants to manage me. There's nothing to manage but my cat and my laundry.

KAT: He likes Florida.

VIC: He's fucking golfing. Can you believe that?

KAT: He says you're making new music.

VIC: That's Bill's story

KAT: You're not?

VIC: Well it's not "new". What's new? Nothing's new.

KAT: It's acoustic he said. You were always talking about doing that. I'd love to hear it. Do you have a copy with you?

VIC: No.

KAT: What you should be doing is working on a website. That's key now. Actually I was thinking of you. We're looking for some themes for a couple of programs. It's great money and it's easy.

VIC: "Themes".

KAT: Theme music for a couple of programs.

VIC: Jingles?

KAT: No, themes. Lots of people do it.

VIC: And lots of people give blow jobs for crack.

KAT's Blackberry vibrates. She turns it off and puts it in her bag. A moment. KAT sees VIC's book on the table.

KAT: You're reading?

VIC: Yeah.

KAT: You finally learned how.

VIC: Ha.

KAT: *(Reading the title.)* The Spirituality of Imperfection. OK.

VIC: "OK"?

KAT: What?

VIC: What do you mean "OK"?

KAT: Nothing. OK. Whatever.

VIC: "Whatever"?

KAT: What? Yeah.

VIC: Yeah what?

KAT: Yeah. What? Nothing.

VIC: Nothing?

KAT: Yeah. Nothing. Good for you.

VIC: Good for me what?

KAT: If that stuff works for you.

VIC: "That stuff".

KAT: That Jesus stuff.

VIC: It's not Jesus.

KAT: No I know, I mean—

VIC: It's not Billy Graham.

KAT: I didn't say it was.

VIC: But you might as well have. Just that—your attitude.

KAT: My attitude?

VIC: Your attitude, this restaurant. What the fuck is this place? Fucking quail? Fifteen dollar potato soup?

An hour late?

KAT: Forty-five minutes.

VIC: I thought it was fifteen?

KAT: You said forty-five.

VIC: Yeah but you said fifteen and now you're saying forty-five.

KAT: Because you said forty-five.

VIC: It was actually a fucking hour.

KAT: You were early, when have you ever been early? It's not my fault you were early.

VIC: It's not your fault, no. It's never your fault. Just like in London.

KAT: Oh please, that's my fault? You're the one who disappeared. How do you think that made me feel?

VIC: Made you feel? Made you feel? You you you it's still all you.

KAT: Take a look at yourself.

VIC: You're talking to me? With your attitude, and your "rebranding the network" and your, what, two thousand dollar sweater. How much did that sweater cost? And your "I know the chef". Laying the bullshit on just like always. And offering me jingle work? Give me a break. I didn't show up to eat your disrespect for dinner.

KAT: So why did you show up?

VIC: I don't know. Maybe because I thought I'd get an apology.

KAT: For what?

VIC: "For what".

KAT: OK, I'm sorry.

VIC: What for?

KAT: Whatever you want me to be sorry for.

VIC: Let's start with being late and work backwards.

KAT: I'm sorry I was late.

VIC: Who's forty-five minutes late by accident? Who?

KAT: Like you were never late. Like you're perfect.

VIC: Fuck you.

KAT: Fuck you.

They stop. VIC immediately regrets her outburst.

VIC: Oh shit.

KAT: We're baaaaack.

VIC: Yeah.

A moment.

KAT: *(Re book.)* How's the spirituality going?

VIC: So so. I'm pretty good with the imperfection though.

KAT: I'm sorry I was late.

VIC: There is a solution.

KAT: What?

VIC: Get a watch.

KAT: Yeah.

VIC: I gotta wash my hands.

VIC rises and leaves. KAT has a moment alone. KAT looks around the restaurant at the TROPHY WIVES and the TABLE OF BUSINESSMEN who are now drunk and laughing.

WAITER 1 passes with a glass of scotch on a tray. KAT speaks to WAITER 1.

KAT: Excuse me?

WAITER 1 stops. KAT takes the scotch from the tray and bangs it back in one. She then breathes a long burst of fire and rises from the table pushing WAITER 1 out of her way.

12 INT. CANOE RESTAURANT / HALLWAY - DAY

We follow behind VIC as she walks down a hallway looking for the washroom. She can't find it, she has passed it, she turns and heads back, she quickens her pace, we follow her, she finds the door and quickly enters.

13 INT. CANOE RESTAURANT - DAY

KAT moves smoothly toward the table of BUSINESSMEN, one MAN sees her coming and rises toward her with a hungry smile.

14 INT. CANOE RESTAURANT / LADIES ROOM - DAY

In seconds VIC has the door locked, her belt off, her jacket sleeve up and is tying off.

15 INT. CANOE RESTAURANT - DAY

KAT grabs the MAN and begins making out on the table, a SECOND MAN approaches to get in on the action.

16 INT. CANOE RESTAURANT / LADIES ROOM - DAY

Close on: VIC pulling loaded needle toward her tied off arm.

SICK VIC: Go for it.

VIC looks over and sees SICK VIC standing nearby. SICK VIC smiles.

What difference does it make now right? There's a juicy vein.

17 INT. CANOE RESTAURANT - DAY

Moments before. KAT sits at the table, the WAITER with the tray and scotch stands before her.

WAITER: Yes?

KAT: Can I get a coffee when you get a chance?

The WAITER departs. KAT looks over at the table of BUSINESSMEN. They pay no notice of her.

18 INT. CANOE RESTAURANT / LADIES ROOM - DAY

VIC looks at herself in the mirror. Back to normal, calmer. She gets down on her knees and she prays.

19 INT. CANOE RESTAURANT - DAY

Later. The meal has finally arrived. KAT eats her quail gently while VIC tears into her salad with a knife and fork.

VIC: I know why you're here.

KAT: I told you why I'm here.

VIC: No, why you're really here.

KAT: And why am I really here?

VIC: I don't need your help OK.

KAT: My help?

VIC: A job or whatever. And don't try to slip any cash in my pocket when I'm not looking. I'm fine. I've got what I need.

KAT: And what's that?

VIC: To do the next right thing, and maintain a conscious connection with my higher power. Just like the book says.

KAT: So do you pray?

VIC: Do I pray?

KAT: *(Sarcastically.)* Get down on your knees and humble yourself before your Higher Power?

VIC: Not with that attitude I don't.

KAT: I'm curious. Give me the "More About Alcoholism" talk.

VIC: Read the book.

KAT: I've read the book.

VIC: I've lived the book.

KAT: Anyway, it's probably different for addicts.

VIC: Not really, a drunk is just a messier junkie.

KAT: I guess.

VIC: Not you though, you're terminally unique.

KAT: Uh huh. As I said, I've read the book.

VIC: You don't do meetings?

KAT: I do meetings.

VIC: But you don't pray?

KAT: I'm more of an agnostic thananything else.

VIC: Yeah well so am I. That's just questioning. Agnostic means "I don't know". Who isn't an agnostic? Who can say they know?

KAT: I've met a few.

VIC: I'm more into the whole philosophical stuff anyway. Like us, as punks, we were Aristotelians—lovers of truth and beauty. But I mean you want to go back—I mean you want to really go back, it was Socrates who really got the whole Aristotelian thing going. Aristotle put the package together but when you really look at it, it was Socrates who lived it. And that's what we were, we were punks in the carpe diem of rock and roll. We took the life we had today and lived it like we'd be dead tomorrow. We were Aristotelians.

KAT: You've been doing your research.

VIC: I've been reading.

KAT: Wikipedia is a wonderful thing.

VIC: *(Smiling.)* Fuck you.

VIC watches as KAT eats her quail. She has her knife in her right hand and her fork in her left, she cuts the quail and takes a piece to her mouth without switching hands.

When'd you start to eat like that?

KAT: I always ate like this. Like what?

VIC: You used to eat like me.

KAT: With my fork in my fist like a spear?

VIC: I don't—

KAT: With my hands?

VIC: No! You used to switch like me.

KAT: Switch?

VIC: Switch, switch! Like switch.

VIC shows her: VIC cuts a tomato with her knife in her right hand, her fork in her left. When she gets a piece of tomato on her fork she puts her knife down and switches her fork to her right hand and takes the tomato to her mouth.

Switch!

KAT: I didn't switch.

VIC: You switched.

KAT: I didn't switch. I was well raised.

VIC: *(Laughing.)* "Well raised."

KAT: It's the proper way to eat.

VIC: You weren't well raised.

KAT: Yes I was. And so were you. You want to go back, that's what I go back to. Our fathers went to work every morning in their Oldsmobiles and our mothers stayed home and ironed the napkins and made macaroni casserole. That's how it was. We weren't Arista-whatevers or Socretians. We weren't even punks. We were dissatisfied middle-class white girls trying to be something we saw in a magazine. We were playing rock-and-roll house. At least we were honest about it then.

VIC: My mother never ironed our napkins.

KAT: But she made an excellent macaroni casserole.

After a moment VIC smiles. She toasts with her tap water.

VIC: To macaroni casserole.

KAT: How about… *(Raising to toast.)* We agnostics.

VIC: *(Toasting.)* We agnostics.

VIC attempts not to "switch" while eating. It feels too weird. She goes back to "switching".

20 INT. CANOE RESTAURANT - DUSK 20

Later. Dusk has descended. KAT sits with a second cup of coffee, VIC eats cake.

KAT: I wish I could eat cake.

VIC: So that's what a wild night on the town has come down to: cake.

KAT: Why, are you looking for a wild night on the town?

VIC: That's not even funny.

KAT: Who's laughing.

WAITER 1 passes.

VIC: The bill?

KAT: I'm just kidding.

VIC: You went from not laughing to kidding pretty quick.

A moment. KAT looks over at one of the TROPHY WIVES still hanging in there but very drunk.

KAT: Her. *(Indicates one of the wives; VIC looks over.)* What's her story?

VIC: I don't know.

KAT: Come on, we used to do that all the time.

VIC: You go ahead.

KAT: Born in Windsor, on the border, smart girl in school but too pretty to be taken seriously. Loved dancing around the basement rec room to "Brother Love's Travelling Salvation Show" and "Brandy".

Won some beauty contest her mother insisted she enter, never liked the beauty part but liked the attention. Bought *Tapestry*. Considered joining the Peace Corps but by the time she was out of high school she just gave in and bought an Olivia NewtonJohn album and decided to get by on her looks. Started going to Detroit on weekends where the bouncers would let her into bars. Heard "Edge of Seventeen" for the first time and it almost changed her life but then she met some rich guy who said he'd take care of her. After he cheated on her the third time she vowed off rich guys and started to listening to Aerosmith. Went to college for hotel management, maybe interior design. Torn between Alannah Myles and Taylor Dayne. At a sports bar she met a blue collar guy with a dog and a truck, they danced to the *Rock and Roll Animal* version of "Sweet Jane" and fell in love, she quit school, they moved in together. But real life is just too hard, all she thinks about is how much easier it would be with a rich guy. She leaves the guy with the truck and buys her first Celine Dion CD and every time she'd listen to it she'd cry about missing the dog. Then she starts going to rich guy bars, she meets one and marries him and pretty soon she realizes she can't stand the rich guy so to get back at him she spends all day every day shopping and then gets drunk with her girlfriends. Some of those days she listens to Aerosmith for an hour then calls up the guy with the truck and they get together for hot sex in some hotel. After sex the guy talks about getting back together, she just smiles and wants to leave. Later she sits in her car in the hotel parking lot and listens to *Rumours* all the way through twice and doesn't feel anything.

She worries that her heart's gotten hard but then feels better when she realizes she still misses the dog.

VIC: Maybe.

KAT: Just maybe?

VIC takes a look at the WIFE.

VIC: It wasn't *Rumours,* it was *Frampton Comes Alive.*

KAT: Of course.

VIC: And she doesn't miss the dog.

KAT: No?

VIC: All she's missing is another martini.

VIC and KAT watch the WIFE.

The WIFE calls WAITER 1 over, it is clear she is very drunk and ordering another drink.

VIC and KAT find this too familiar and depressing.

And that is how it works.

KAT: Come with me?

VIC: Alright. But I'm not doing anything.

KAT smiles and rises to leave. VIC follows her.

I said I wasn't doing anything. Did you hear me when I said that. I'm not doing anything.

21 INT. ELEVATOR - NIGHT

VIC and KAT ride down in the elevator. Muzak plays.

KAT: I'd like to change.

VIC: Your clothes?

KAT: Yes.

VIC: You look fine.

KAT: I look like I work in television.

VIC: You do work in television.

KAT: I just want to change.

VIC: Oh please. You're not going to wear the two thousand dollar sweater? You probably bought it for tonight.

KAT: It wasn't two thousand dollars.

VIC: One thousand.

KAT: No.

VIC: Nine hundred.

KAT: No. Lend me something. Let's go to your place and I'll wear something of yours.

VIC: You want to wear something of mine?

KAT: We used to. And I'd like to see your place.

VIC: Mmmmm.

KAT: Why not?

VIC: I wasn't expecting a guest from L.A.

KAT: I'm not "from" L.A., I just live there. I'm from here. I'm from down the street and around the corner from you.

VIC: Not in a nine hundred dollar sweater you're not.

KAT: It wasn't nine hundred dollars.

VIC: Eight-fifty?

KAT says nothing.

Bingo.

KAT: I want to change.

VIC: Alright. And you can say hi to Brian.

KAT laughs at what she thinks is a hilarious joke. VIC looks at her with a "What?"

KAT: You're kidding.

22 INT. APARTMENT / KITCHEN - NIGHT

BRIAN, 40s, VIC's long time boyfriend, sits at small desk jammed into a corner of the kitchen of the tiny apartment. He wears a housecoat and eats a bowl of cereal. He has been working on the computer and has turned to face KAT. KAT stands awkwardly nearby.

BRIAN: So.

KAT: So yeah.

BRIAN: How have you been?

KAT: Good.

BRIAN: Good.

KAT: Yeah.

BRIAN: Would you like a bowl of cereal?

KAT: Uh. No thanks we just had dinner.

BRIAN: OK. Well. I better get back to my novel.

KAT: You're writing a novel?

BRIAN: It's more of a memoir.

KAT: Oh.

BRIAN: It's either called "The Average Life of a Magnificent Man" or "The Magnificent Life of an Average Man."

KAT: They're both…

BRIAN: Compelling.

KAT: Yeah.

BRIAN: Yeah. *(Confidentially.)* And don't worry, it won't be full disclosure.

KAT: Oh.

BRIAN: So no worries.

KAT: Oh…

VIC calls from the other room.

VIC: *(O.S.)* The only thing clean are T-shirts.

KAT: I'll take a T-shirt.

23 INT. APARTMENT / LIVING ROOM - NIGHT

A few minutes later. KAT has put on a pair of VIC's jeans and a Lynyrd Skynyrd T-shirt. KAT takes in the messy room with its college student vibe. VIC walks into the room.

VIC: Oh.

KAT: What?

VIC: Now we're dressed the same.

KAT: Lot's of people wear ironic T-shirts.

VIC: Why is Lynyrd Skynyrd ironic?

KAT: I mean a band T-shirt is ironic.

VIC: Why?

KAT: In its youthfulness.

VIC: I'm going to put something else on.

KAT: Wear my sweater.

VIC considers this a moment.

VIC: Yeah, alright, I'll wear your sweater.

VIC leaves the room. BRIAN appears in the doorway singing"Free Bird".

BRIAN: Skynyrd. Suits you.

KAT: *(Uncomfortable.)*.Thanks.

BRIAN: Ah sweet memories.

KAT: Sometimes.

KAT follows after VIC. BRIAN continues his heartfelt "Free Bird".

24 EXT. QUEEN STREET WEST - NIGHT

We hear the band Metric playing a balls-out version of "Free Bird". We see the glitter and the dirt of Queen Street West. It's all slo-mo rock 'n roll as VIC and KAT walk down the sidewalk. They take in their surroundings: the trashed out hipsters in front of the Bovine Sex Club, the anorexic wannabes lined up for Ultra Supper Club, the desperados outside the Salvation Army Shelter, the cowboys and artists outside the Cameron House, all of it, everything and everyone touched by the glow of the imagined beauty and depravity of the coolest street in the world. The girls are here and they are owning it.

Suddenly everything goes back to real time when VIC nearly bumps into a LOST SOUL off her meds.

LOST SOUL: Which way is Spadina?

VIC: One block east.

LOST SOUL: Does the Spadina bus go to heaven?

VIC: I don't know. It didn't for me.

Back in normal time the street has the elements as above but more reality: marauding frat boys, crack heads doing their crack walk hustle, immigrant students with their laundry, runaways and overweight shoppers from the burbs.

25 EXT. QUEEN STREET WEST - NIGHT

VIC and KAT are walking across the street from the Bovine Sex Club. KAT stops and watches the small line of freaks and fuckups outside the club. VIC stops and watches with her.

KAT: What do they want?

VIC: What does anybody want?

KAT: No they're different. Other people want white teeth and clean sheets and low interest rates. They don't want that.

VIC takes a moment to observe them.

VIC: The boys want to get laid and the girls want true love. Just like the magazines tell them they should.

KAT: The boys don't want true love?

VIC: Neither do the girls really, but that's how everybody ends up getting laid.

VIC walks on. After a moment KAT follows.

26 EXT. QUEEN STREET WEST - NIGHT

Steady-cam shot as we walk along with VIC and KAT as they talk.

KAT: This is good. This is great. This is like a vacation.

Some people want a view, some people want the sunrise on the lake, some people want an island in the South Pacific. This my vacation. To be down in all this.

VIC: I can't afford this kind of vacation.

KAT: I'm just looking.

VIC: I've already got what I'm looking for.

KAT: Brian?

VIC: It's comfortable.

KAT: You love him?

VIC: Love is a minefield, love is a…

KAT: Battlefield?

VIC: This is love: I secretly believe that I'm unlovable and then I meet you. You say you love me. I love you because you love me. But that has nothing to do with you, it's about you loving me, I only love you because I imagine myself unlovable and you, against all odds love me. And then at some point you do something that makes me think you don't love me, which I'm more ready to believe than you loving me because I'm unlovable. So I stop loving you because I only love you because you love me and I'm unlovable.

KAT: What about the other person?

VIC: Who?

KAT: The person who loves you?

VIC: No no, it's the same thing, everybody's doing the same thing.

KAT: Why?

VIC: Because everybody thinks they're unlovable too.

KAT: I'm not unlovable. I'm all lovable. I am the very meaning of lovable.

VIC: Oh yeah you believe that.

KAT: Just because you're living in the shadows doesn't mean some of us aren't walking in the sunshine.

VIC: We block the sunshine to make the shadow.

KAT: How "Go Ask Alice".

VIC: People think love will complete them. See what people really want is to feel complete. What people really want is peace of mind.

KAT: Take another little piece of my heart now baby.

VIC: Peace of mind is the ticket. That's all I ever wanted and everything I did to get it got me farther away from it. I never did the one thing I needed to do.

KAT: Head transplant?

VIC: Into action, into action, into action.

KAT: So we're back to the battlefield?

VIC: I used to sit around waiting for it to come tap me on the shoulder. "Hey there, come with me." Or for something to descend upon me and lift me up out of my shit. But no. I had to do the work. And you know when the work started? When I stopped waiting for someone to love me.

KAT: Sounds to me like you're running away.

VIC: From what?

KAT: Ghosts. The future. Ghosts of the future.

KAT steps away. VIC stops and looks across the street.

SICK VIC stands in front of a bar. SICK VIC waves to VIC.

VIC moves quickly to catch up to KAT.

28 EXT. GREAT HALL - NIGHT 28

VIC and KAT stand outside the Great Hall. A line has formed. They stand apart from the line up. Nearby a GROUP OF ROCKER CHICKS stand handing a flask around.

VIC: I don't know. I think I may just head.

KAT: What's the problem?

VIC looks around at the groups gathered outside the venue.

VIC: Nothing's changed. It's just like yesterday.

KAT: Tomorrow was always just yesterday in disguise as today. It's all yesterday.

VIC: I never liked yesterday.

KAT: You were just scared of it.

VIC: What were you scared of?

KAT: You.

VIC: Me too.

KAT: Look you can either be in the world or be out of the world. If you want to be in the world it's right in there, if you want to be out of the world you can go back to your apartment and eat cereal with Brian. But good luck selling records that way.

VIC: "Records"? I didn't know people still sold records.

KAT: They're downloading, but there's still cash involved. Come on in and see what they're buying.

VIC: I don't know.

KAT: You're safe with me baby, I'm lovable enough for both of us.

VIC: I'm not standing in line.

KAT: Let me see if I can find somebody.

KAT steps off. VIC looks around at the GROUP OF ROCKER CHICKS. They are a little drunk, they laugh and shove one another.

ROCKER CHICK 1: This sucks.

ROCKER CHICK 2: You suck.

ROCKER CHICK 3: You suck worse.

ROCKER CHICK 4: This whole scene sucks.

ROCKER CHICK 1: This whole city sucks.

ROCKER CHICK 2: This whole planet sucks.

ROCKER CHICK 3: I am suck.

ROCKER CHICK 4: Suck is.

ROCKER CHICK 1 notices VIC.

ROCKER CHICK 1: Hey are you Vic from Trigger. *(VIC looks at her.)* You're Vic from Trigger.

VIC: No. Sorry.

ROCKER CHICK 1: You sure?

VIC: Pretty much yeah.

KAT calls from the door of the venue.

KAT: Vic?

The ROCKER CHICK turns to her friends.

ROCKER CHICK 1: It is! It's Vic from Trigger!

The ROCKER CHICKS gather.

VIC: Listen—

ROCKER CHICK 2 drops to the ground.

ROCKER CHICK 2: Let me just touch the bottom of your shoe!

VIC: No.

VIC gives the ROCKER CHICK her hand to help her up.

ROCKER CHICK 2: I just touched Vic from Trigger's hand!

The ROCKER CHICK 3 pulls a cassette out of her bag and holds it out tentatively to VIC.

ROCKER CHICK 3: Would you listen to our band?

VIC: A cassette?

ROCKER CHICK 3: You want a CD?

VIC: No no a cassette's OK, I like cassettes.

ROCKER CHICK 4: Yeah me too. Fuck digital, "Piss Flap" doesn't go digital.

VIC: "Piss Flap"?

ROCKER CHICK 4: Yeah.

VIC: Catchy.

ROCKER CHICK 1: Bill Gates can keep his hands off Piss Flap.

VIC takes the cassette and heads toward the venue.

29 INT. GREAT HALL - NIGHT

The Hall is packed with people, many of them women. The concert has begun and interspersed through the next several scenes is something of a mini concert film. The following series of scenes are bracketed by performances from the stage.

KAT and VIC make their way through the crowd and backstage.

30 INT. GREAT HALL / GREEN ROOM - NIGHT

KAT and VIC stand on their own in the green room near the food and drink table. There are a LOT OF PEOPLE, some musicians but mostly press, friends and hangers-on. KAT and VIC don't know anyone and no one seems to know them but VIC is energized by the encounter with the ROCKER CHICK outside and is enjoying the vibe. KAT is not liking feeling anonymous. She is also annoyed by the free bar and the happy drinkers. It's all a bit too much for her. She hunches her shoulders and keeps her head down. VIC is loving the energy in the room. The music is loud from the stage.

VIC: This isn't so bad.

KAT: In what way?

A CRAZY GIRL, screaming into her cell phone pushes past KAT and grabs a bottle of Jager from the table.

CRAZY GIRL: We're going to get fucked up!

KAT looks like she might tear a strip off the CRAZY GIRL.

VIC: The tribe has gathered and the natives are restless.

BILLY appears behind VIC, wearing an "industry" laminate.

BILLY: If this is the tribe then you're the chief.

VIC: Billy, hey there asshole.

BILLY: You're looking good Vicky.

BILLY nods to KAT.

Kat.

KAT: Bill. Scouting some talent?

BILLY: Stalking Miss Vic.

VIC: How's Florida?

BILLY: Like Thunder Bay but hot and with tourists.

VIC: *(To KAT.)* He's fucking golfing can you believe it.

BILLY: It's cheaper than a shrink and less crowded than meetings.

VIC: You and Alice Cooper. Golfing.

BILLY: Don't laugh, apparently he shoots. Listen Vicky the boys from EMI are keen to meet. Ball's in your court.

VIC: Yeah yeah, I'm thinking about it.

KAT: I'm going to check out the band.

BILLY: *(To KAT.)* How's L.A.?

KAT: L.A.

BILLY: Are you staying out of trouble?

KAT: Do I look like I'm staying out of trouble?

BILLY: Yeah. But you were always good at disguises.

KAT: Don't worry about me.

KAT departs.

BILLY: *(To VIC re KAT.)* Keep an eye on that one.

VIC: Yeah?

BILLY: Something's in the air.

VIC: Catch you later.

VIC departs. The CRAZY GIRL approaches BILLY.

CRAZY GIRL: Oh my God, you're him!

BILLY: Oh my God, you're an idiot.

The CRAZY GIRL departs pissed.

31 INT. GREEN ROOM- NIGHT

KAT is about to leave the room. VIC stops her.

VIC: Hey. What's up?

KAT: Nothing. I don't know. I'm not feeling this scene.

VIC: It's not so bad.

KAT: You got a little attention.

VIC: What?

KAT: I saw that kid talking to you outside. And the boys from EMI are keen to meet.

VIC: Whatever.

KAT: Doesn't take much to wake up your ego

VIC: It's not about my ego. It just... I've got this music coming out and I was... I've been asking myself why, you know. What's the point of another song, the world's caving in on itself and half the planet's expecting the Second Coming.

KAT: Maybe that's what you can call the CD.

VIC: No listen, I'm saying— What I'm saying is whole thing is a together thing. The gathering. Working with others, right? That's all it's about, that's what matters. It's not the music it's who the music brings together. That's what we're looking for.

KAT: And your twelve songs of acoustic introspection are going to bring the whole world together.

VIC: What? What are you talking about?That's not what I'm saying.

KAT: Maybe you can go out and do one of your new songs tonight.

VIC: What? "Acoustic introspection"? What's that supposed to mean? You haven't even heard it. What happened to turn you into such a bitch all of a sudden?

KAT: Look just don't look for depth in this scene OK. It's all just the same superficial shit it always was. And it's even worse now than it was then.

VIC: It's still rock and roll.

KAT: Rock and roll is just a scent, you pick it up in the air and it reminds you of something. It's just an odour.

VIC: Whatever. Let's go smell the band.

VIC leads KAT out of the room.

32 INT. BACKSTAGE - NIGHT

KAT and VIC watch a band finish a number. VIC hoots appreciation. KAT is less than impressed.

HILLARY the stage manager appears carrying a clipboard and wearing a headset.

HILLARY: *(To VIC and KAT.)* Don't move.

(To crowd.) Alright people, this is basically stage area.

I'm looking for laminates that say full access, if I don't see a laminate with the words "FULL ACCESS" you are out front with the regular folks.

KAT: We're…

HILLARY: Oh God no I know. You're Trigger. Huge fan huge fan. You made high school less than hell. I bow down. But tonight it's business.

(To crowd.) Laminates people!

(To KAT.) And thanks for putting this together.

VIC: What?

KAT: *(To VIC.)* No, for being part of this she means.

HILLARY: *(To KAT.)* I thought you were on the board.

KAT: The board? No no, no way. How boring. Who has

time? We're just here. To be here. Happy to be here.

HILLARY: Sorry. Right. So will you guys be performing?

KAT: She's not but I might.

VIC: What?

KAT: Or she might do something acoustic from her new stuff.

HILLARY: We can squeeze you in after Carole Pope does Anne Murray.

VIC: *(To HILLARY.)* She's being a comedian.

KAT: Yeah, for sure I'm going to play.

VIC: Who are you going to play with?

HILLARY: You could play with Foxfire.

KAT: Perfect. When?

HILLARY: Now.

KAT: Oh. Sure. Yeah.

HILLARY: Great. It's done.

HILLARY gets on her headset and leads KAT to the stage. KAT gives VIC the finger as she leaves. HILLARY turns back to VIC.

(To VIC.) I bow down.

VIC: Save it for Carole Pope.

HILLARY: *(Swooning.)* I know! *(To crowd.)* Watch your backs!

VIC watches as KAT walks out on stage. The band Foxfire is setting up. They greet her and laugh together.

On stage HANNAH the lead singer hands KAT a guitar as the other band members take their places. They talk about what song to play, they consult with KAT and she agrees.

KAT fingers the guitar, the strap, she adjusts it to her liking. She takes in the view from the stage. All is silent but her breathing. The crowd is yelling for the band to start but all we hear is her measured breaths. She tries to settle in. She is nervous but finally gives over to a feeling of home. Slowly the sounds of the room trickle back to being heard. She's missed this.

VIC watches KAT on stage. She is torn between nostalgia and envy, wanting not to care but caring despite herself. The CRAZY GIRL and TWO FRIENDS are drunk and screaming close by. Then someone speaks to VIC.

SICK VIC: *(O.C.)* What a cunt.

VIC turns and sees SICK VIC standing beside her watching KAT on stage.

Look at her, so fucking full of herself, what a bitch. Doesn't it just twist your fucking tits. Look at her with those fucking kids, it's musical pedophilia. Fucking obscene. What a piece of shit.What do you suppose that fucking haircut cost? Fucking save Darfur with what that haircut cost. Turns my stomach just to look at that waste of oxygen. And that bitch is talking to you about ego? What do you know about ego? You crushed up your ego with baby laxative and snorted it long ago. You wouldn't know Ego if Ego herself strapped on the CN Tower and bent you over.

On stage HANNAH heads for the mic.

HANNAH: So how are you foxy bitches doing tonight?

The crowd cheers.

Tonight we've got a special—

HANNAH is about to introduce KAT, she looks at KAT and KAT catches her eye shaking her head no. HANNAH gets it.

Yeah so tonight we've got a special song in tribute of all the girls in the room.

The band comes down hard into "Standing Alongside Gone" a song that has both the grace of KAT and the edge of VIC. KAT hangs back at first but then gets into it. Soon she is the KAT of old, sharing vocals with HANNAH.

Slowly the crowd becomes aware of KAT's presence on stage. Much of the room moves toward the stage wanting to get close to what they feel is an historic moment.

On stage KAT lets herself go. She's into it like it was yesterday.

In the wings:

SICK VIC: Have a drink for fuck's sake.

VIC: Shut up.

SICK VIC: I mean what's the point right. Have a drink.

VIC: Shut up.

SICK VIC: *(Mocking her.)* "Shut up." "Shut up." Sorry Ma'am. Hope I didn't offend you. You weakling. You're such a fucking lightweight it makes me laugh. You make her look pretty fucking good when it comes down to it. At least she hasn't cashed in all her chips.

At least she's still got a fucking job. You and your fucking shame and your fucking apologies, your fucking "making amends." Bullshit.

VIC moves away disturbed, crossing in front of the CRAZY GIRL. The CRAZY GIRL is annoyed by VIC momentarily blocking her view. VIC takes a breath. SICK VIC is beside her once again.

Maybe you"re sober but you're still one mighty self-satisfied asshole.

VIC moves back to her earlier position. The CRAZY GIRL is annoyed again.

From the stage KAT notices that VIC is moving uncomfortably around the wings. KAT keeps an eye on VIC.

Standing by herself VIC takes a couple of deep breaths. SICK VIC is with her again. SICK VIC takes out a piece of tinfoil and fires up a lighter underneath it.

How long are you going to keep this up? "Give over," "give over," it's just a matter of time anyway. Your music sucks, your liver's fucked, and you think you've got another chance? You're dreaming. All that hard work, all those prayers, all those meetings and where does it get you? Dead.

SICK VIC inhales the smoking shit off the tinfoil with a straw. She holds her breath as she speaks.

Ooo that's nice.

SICK VIC holds out the tinfoil and straw to VIC. SICK VIC exhales in VIC's face.

Gimme a kiss.

VIC in one movement swats the tinfoil out of SICK VIC's hand and pushes her away. With this action VIC bumps into the CRAZY GIRL who in turn falls into her friends.

The CRAZY GIRL goes crazy and rushes to attack

VIC. Her friends get in on the action, one pulling at VIC and the other trying to hold the CRAZY GIRL back.

From KAT's perspective on the stage it looks to her like VIC is starting a fight with the CRAZY GIRL and her friends.

Suddenly the wing is filled with people both getting in on and trying to stop the scuffle. VIC manages to find her way out of the melee. She rushes onto the stage for safety.

When VIC arrives on stage the crowd goes wild, recognizing her. KAT hands her the guitar. KAT yells something in VIC's ear but VIC can't hear her. Not knowing what else to do VIC starts playing. Quickly VIC is into it. HANNAH and the band back off a bit and VIC and KAT take over vocals on the song.The crowd goes wild.

In the wing the fight has spread beyond the CRAZY GIRL. Now two SECURITY GUARDS are there. One is trying to break up the fight and the other speaks with the CRAZY GIRL and her friend.

From the stage KAT notices what's happening in the wings.

The CRAZY GIRL and her friend both point toward VIC on the stage. The SECURITY GUARD looks at VIC.

KAT gets VIC's attention. VIC looks into the wing. The SECURITY GUARD motions for VIC to come back to talk to him. VIC ignores him. The SECURITY GUARD speaks into his headset.VIC and KAT notice TWO SECURITY GUARDS at the front of the stage in the crowd responding to a call on their headsets. They both turn and look up at VIC. They move to climb up on the stage. The SECURITY GUARD in the wing also steps toward VIC.

VIC wanting to avoid this confrontation at all costs grabs KAT by the arm and leads her off the stage quickly and into the other wing.

VIC pauses a moment and runs back to the mic.

VIC: *(On mic; to the crowd.)* Thank you Edmonton!

She rushes off stage with KAT.

33 EXT. GREAT HALL - NIGHT

KAT and VIC rush out of the stage door and quickly down the street and into a Park.

KAT keeps looking back to see if they're being followed while VIC keeps moving forward frightened and spinning with excitement.

KAT: Why are we running away?

VIC: I'm on probation.

KAT: For what?

VIC: Shit happens. It wasn't me.

KAT: Right.

VIC: Those bitches went OFF. That was like dropping a match in a gas station.

KAT: What are you doing dropping matches?

VIC: It wasn't me.

KAT: Of course not.

VIC runs into the park. KAT stops.

I can't go in there with these shoes.

VIC: Then take off the fucking shoes.

KAT follows VIC.

KAT: Goddamnit. This kind of shit is no fun sober.

34 EXT. ALLAN GARDENS GREENHOUSE - NIGHT

VIC and KAT approach the greenhouse.

KAT: Where are we going?

VIC: We're going to hide out for awhile and then go to the after party.

KAT: You're not serious.

VIC: I'm going to mess that crazy bitch up.

KAT: Vic…

VIC: I'm kidding.

KAT: I'm seriously going to have a drink tonight.

VIC stops and looks seriously at KAT.

I'm kidding!

VIC: You don't sound like you're kidding.

VIC breaks a pane of glass in the greenhouse window and opens the door. VIC enters. KAT follows.

KAT: No wonder you're on probabtion.

VIC: We're all on probation baby.

35 INT. GREENHOUSE - NIGHT

VIC and KAT walk through the greenhouse. They are quiet, KAT breathes in the green of the space, VIC runs her hands through leaves as she walks along.

36 INT. GREENHOUSE - NIGHT

VIC and KAT are mellow as they sit in a corner of the greenhouse. VIC reaches into her pocket and takes out the cassette. She hands it to KAT.

KAT: *(Reading the cassette.)* "Piss Flap?"

VIC: Poor kid.

KAT: I'll give it a listen.

KAT tucks in into her pocket.

(Laughing.) "Piss Flap."

VIC: It's better than "The Shutups."

KAT: *(Laughing.)* Well we were fourteen.

VIC: That was so lame.

KAT: No, "The Shutups" was pure. "The Shutups" was when we were perfect.

A moment.

VIC: I'm tired all the time.

KAT: Yeah I know. I never used to get tired. I never slept. I only ever used to pass out.

VIC: Yeah. Or if I did get tired I'd take a drink or a hit and then I'd click again. Even a nod isn't like being tired. Going into a nod was like the air turning to jello and an emotional flatline but it wasn't like tired.

When I get tired now I think that this is probably how normal people feel. This is as close to normie as I'm every going to get.

KAT: Life's too short to get tired.

A moment.

"Life is short and…something's long." What do they say? "Life is short but hell is long." That's what my grandmother used to say.

VIC: Hell. I don't know if it's long but it's deep.

KAT: Deep and dark.

VIC: Dark and deep and deep and dark and deep and dark and deep.

KAT: And dark.

VIC: And deep.

KAT looks up through the greenhouse ceiling into the dark sky above.

KAT: I once heard someone at a meeting say "They opened the gates and I thought I was getting let into heaven but it turned out I was getting let out of hell."

VIC: That's good.

KAT: But it's all dark and deep isn't it.

VIC looks up as well. After a moment:

VIC: You know what started it for me? The real beginning of the descent?

Love. That Scottish guy I met in London, when I left the tour? All fucked up and beautiful? Or maybe he was just beautiful because he was fucked up. And he knew how fucked up he was, like I did. Sometimes it was like looking in a mirror. He'd get that same look in his eyes. I could see what he was doing to himself and I wanted to help him. More than wanting to party with him I wanted to help him, and that's what made me think it was love. And it was. It doesn't matter how long you know someone, you can give them your heart in a minute, your soul. And we did. And we were going to help one another stay clean. And we did for awhile. I'd slip and he'd be there to catch me, and I'd do that for him too. But then it only took one time, once, we hit it together. It was a free fall. His uncle or someone had an apartment in Paris but the uncle lived in Dubai or somefuckwhere. We stayed there for a month and by the end of it we didn't talk to anyone but the dealers who would come by. We were so bad one dealer started calling to check on us. And the deeper we got the more connected we were. And it wasn't the drugs, it wasn't the fuckup that was killing us, it was the love. I had split myself open from the neck to the waist and pried my ribs apart and he crawled in; and he did the same and I crawled in to him. One inside the other inside the other. We were this one person, this new organism. It was like we were the mirror, and then we scraped off the back, the stuff that holds the reflection, and crushed it up and cooked it and shot it. Everything was dead but the love and the love was death and it never said a word but it was the loudest thing you ever heard. It was over for me, it was the end. I was waking up disappointed that I was still alive.

But all the time I had in my head,way deep in the back of my head that me dying meant he would too. And maybe that's what saved me, knowing it was the only way to save him. One morning in Paris… The apartment was in this alley, with another building really close across. And so every morning there was only a small amount of time when there was any sun in the room. At this point where the sun would rise just over the building across on it's way to overhead, there'd be this little lick of sun on the floor, it would last maybe…less than an hour. Most mornings I'd sit in the corner and wait for it and watch it move across the floor and disappear but this one morning it didn't seem to be moving, like it was staying longer, like it was calling to me. And I crawled across the floor, slowly slowly across the floor toward it and I stuck my hand in it. I just laid my hand on the floor in the sunlight and my body soaked it in through my hand and it was like the sunlight went to my brain, went straight to my brain, like I woke up for a minute, like it burnt out all the shit for a minute and my brain told me "go or he'll die". And somehow I got up and I put on some clothes and I left him sleeping on the sofa and I left, and I went out and I found the sun and started walking toward it, like I was trying to walk into it. Thinking "go go go, go or he'll die". I never went back.

KAT: What was his name? Something Scottish.

VIC: Mark.

KAT: Oh.

VIC: But he said it in that Scottish way. "Mark".

KAT: What happened to him?

VIC stares into the sky a long moment. She says nothing.

So that's love? Leaving people is love?

VIC: I guess, a kind of love.

KAT: Is that what happened with us?

A moment.

To me love isn't something you leave because it's not something you're "in". That's just the love that gets radio play. And it's not something that crawls up inside you. That's just the love they make movies about.

VIC: So what is it then?

KAT: I don't know. I don't know what it is but I know what it isn't. My mother might know. Your mother. They seemed to be able to make it work. The mothers have the answer. The wives.

VIC: "Making it work." Is that love?

KAT: *Making It Work*. No that's a song on the radio. The kind they play on dedication shows late at night.

VIC: To wives.

KAT: "To wives everywhere."

KAT looks into the dark greenhouse, staring at something that isn't there. VIC watches her. They are quiet.

37 EXT. STREET - NIGHT

VIC and KAT emerge from the park and quickly flag and enter a cab.

38 INT. CAB - NIGHT

Getting inside the cab VIC hands the after party invite to the cabbie.

VIC: Take us here.

CABBIE: That's all the way out in the burbs.

VIC: What's the problem, your mommy won't let you take the car that far.

KAT: *(To CABBIE.)* She's being funny. That's OK, we can take another cab.

CABBIE: *(To KAT.)* You I'll take.

VIC: What about me?

CABBIE: *(To VIC.)* You're with her.

The CABBIE puts the car in gear.

VIC: As always.

39 EXT. LAKE SHORE BOULEVARD- NIGHT

MUSIC: Emily Haines "Our Hell." The cab dives along Lake Shore Boulevard.

40 INT. CAB - NIGHT

MUSIC continues. Inside the cab both VIC and KAT are mellow as they slouch into the backseat. VIC looks out her window at the passing lake. KAT looks out her window at the city skyline.

KAT: Can I ask you something?

VIC looks at KAT. KAT continues to look out the window.

VIC: What?

KAT: Who do you pray to?

VIC: I don't know.

KAT: How can you pray if you don't know who to?

VIC: I just pray to whatever's keeping those other assholes sober.

VIC looks away. KAT looks at VIC. She wants to get it but she's not sure she does.

41 EXT./INT. CAB/SUBURBAN NEIGHBORHOODS - NIGHT

Music continues as the cab drives off the expressway and through suburban neighborhoods. KAT and VIC watch the neighborhoods as they pass through them. At first old neighborhoods with large lawns and slightly different houses. Then new developments with cookie-cutter townhouses. It's like a journey from the distant past to the recent past and then finally into the future: secret enclaves of the rich, deep beyond the suburbs, gate after gate, mansion after mansion. The cab finally pulls up in front of a large high school.

42 EXT. HIGH SCHOOL - NIGHT

Outside the high school a VALET parks cars as musical equipment is unloaded from a cube van. The cab pulls up.

43 INT. CAB - NIGHT

KAT and VIC are slightly incredulous.

KAT: Are you sure this is it?

CABBIE: That's what the card says.

VIC: Whatever, let's check it out.

VIC gets out.

KAT: *(To CABBIE.)* Will you wait for us?

CABBIE: How long?

KAT takes a hundred dollar bill from her pocket. She holds it up for the CABBIE.

KAT: This long?

CABBIE: Sure.

He reaches for it. KAT rips it in half and gives him one half.

KAT: We'll be back.

44 INT. HIGH SCHOOL - NIGHT

VIC and KAT walk into the main foyer of the high school. As they walk along they take it all in. A huge CROWD. PRIVILEGED TEENS, who look older and more sophisticated than any teen should, wander about texting on rhinestone encrusted Blackberrys drinking Rockstar and Redbull and champagne with straws from small bottles. ADULTS both HIPSTER and SUIT mingle among the young crowd unselfconsciously.

KAT and VIC enter the gymnasium where on the stage instruments are struck by ROADIES and new ones take their place. UBER-GEEKS record the proceedings on webcams and laptops.

VIC: I don't know.

KAT: I don't know either.

VIC: I hated high school the first time.

KAT: Then why'd you take five years to finish?

VIC: Let's get out of here.

KAT: *(Moving to leave.)* Come on.

A voice approaches.

BEEBEE: *(O.S.)* Well fuck the fuck off.

VIC and KAT turn to face BEEBEE. VIC greets her warmly. BEEBEE is a musician, around the age of VIC and KAT, blonde

BeeBee. Hey doll.

BEEBEE: I didn't think I'd see your mug here. Hi Kat.

KAT: Hi BeeBee.

BEEBEE: *(To KAT.)* You're so thin. You must be on that L.A. diet, bullshit and bottled water.

KAT: That's a good one. You look the same.

BEEBEE: Ouch.

KAT: No, you look good.

BEEBEE: I'm a thousand fucking years old shut up.

(To VIC.) So that was quite the performance.

What did you do to piss off security?

VIC: It wasn't me.

BEEBEE: No I know, never was. Me neither.

VIC: This is the after party?

BEEBEE: Fuck I know. One of the suits thought it would be radical to get fucked up in a high school. It's like "Detroit Rock City" crossed with a Sweet Sixteen. Fucking KISS is probably going to play. Fuck, look at these kids. Thank God I'm not their age now, I'd be dead in a weekend. Come on, come upstairs to the green room, the stalwarts are gathered.

VIC: There's a green room?

BEEBEE: In the science lab.

45 INT. HIGH SCHOOL / SCIENCE LAB - NIGHT

In the science lab, a huge buffet and bar is laid out. The room is surrounded with glowing candles and comfortable chairs and sofas have been placed amid the science worktables. A cluster of MUSICIANS are gathered in a corner around a cooler drinking and blowing smoke out a window. A group of CHILDREN and a SMALL DOG run in and out of the room.

VIC and BEEBEE have joined two male musicians BUCKY and HONEY who engage VIC in familiar conversation.

KAT stands about the periphery. Despite her dressed down look she doesn't feel part of this scene.

BUCKY: Apparently Jeremy took one look at the high school and wouldn't even come up the driveway.

BEEBEE: He was probably scared a bully would steal his bicycle.

HONEY: He's upgraded to a scooter now.

BUCKY: Which he rides all winter. Fucking Canadians.

BEEBEE: Don't you be dissing us beavers.

HONEY: *(To BEEBEE.)* Aren't you Canadian?

BEEBEE: I'm fucking Martian. I'm a Saturnurite. I'm a Plutonian.

Don't listen to him Honey, he's so Canadian he shits loonies.

BUCKY: Maple syrup runs in my veins. If I could find one.

HONEY: *(At cooler; to VIC.)* Beer?

VIC: I'm good.

BEEBEE: She's a very good girl.

HONEY: *(To VIC.)* Toby played me one of the tracks he engineered for you. Really beautiful.

VIC: It's what it is.

HONEY: That's the way to do it. Scale way down. You and a guitar, a piano. Keep it simple.

BEEBEE gives VIC a kiss on the cheek.

BEEBEE: Keep it simple stupid.

KAT notices a YOUNG MOTHER on a sofa nearby breast-feeding her toddler. She stares, lost in this image. The YOUNG MOTHER looks up smiling. KAT looks quickly away embarrassed.

The MUSICIANS continue to talk. KAT wanders away unnoticed.

46 INT. HIGH SCHOOL HALLWAY - NIGHT

KAT goes down the hallway.

47 INT. MUSIC CLASSROOM - NIGHT

KAT stands in the doorway of a classroom. It is blue with moonlight. She steps inside. The room is full of musical equipment and instruments, a piano. She sits at the piano a moment. She considers playing but she doesn't. She rises. She picks up a guitar and puts it down. She feels both at home and alien in this place.

She finds a boombox and takes the "Piss Flap" cassette from her pocket and puts it in the deck. After a few tries she manages to figure out the settings.

The music is pretty much paint-by-numbers punk-lite, not terrible but nothing special, Siouxsie and the Banshsees without the hooks. A KID speaks from the shadows startling KAT.

KID: It's not bad but we're better.

The KID steps out into the light, she looks to be about fourteen, skinny and scruffy and with lots of attitude. She holds a guitar behind her back.

KAT: Oh, you scared me.

KID: What are you doing here?

KAT: I'm…looking around. What are you doing here?

KID: I'm in the band, we're going to play in a minute.

KAT: You're in the band?

KID: Yeah. *(She produces her guitar from behind her back.)* What do you think this is for?

The KID has a joint in her hand, she takes a hit off it.

KAT: How old are you?

KID: Sixteen.

KAT: I doubt that.

KID: How old are you?

KAT: Old enough.

KID: I'd say about fifty.

KAT: Thanks.

The KID offers KAT a hit. She refuses it.

You're a little young to be smoking aren't you?

KID: I guess dropping acid would be easier on my lungs. It's done anyway.

The KID licks her fingers and puts out the roach, saving it in her pocket. The KID watches KAT and has no intention of leaving. KAT watches her a moment.

KAT: *(Re: the music.)* What do you think of this?

KID: They're just trying to sound like Siouxsie and the Banshees.

KAT: Siouxsie and the Banshees?

KID: You never heard of Siouxsie and the Banshees?

KAT: Yeah I've heard of Siouxsie and the Banshees.

The KID strums a bit on the guitar. She's not terrible but no Chrissie Hynde. KAT turns off the music. The KID stops.

And how's your band?

KID: It's just my friend and me right now and a drummer who we're probably going to fire after tonight. We're pretty good.

KAT looks down at a box on the table. It's filled with old 45s. She looks through them.

What are those?

KAT: *(Holding one up.)* You don't know what these are?

KID: Oh yeah. They smash up great when you whiff them at a wall.

KAT: Smash them? You don't smash these, these are holy, these are living history. My first one was… *Fox on the Run* by Sweet.

(She sings the guitar riff.) That guitar is still perfect.

I always wanted albums but they would take my whole allowance. For me these were like candy to a sugar addict waiting for cake. You'd walk into the record store and these would be all on one wall. Some days I couldn't even get past the wall, I couldn't walk into the store where the albums were because I knew I couldn't afford them. It was too painful. But even when I had saved up enough for one it was torture to try and pick just one album. I would spend a whole afternoon wandering up and down the aisles picking them up, turning them over, reading the notes on the sleeves. And then they started putting the notes inside the sleeves and I hated that because then I'd have to buy the album to read it. At first it was just double albums but then even single LP's would have a double sleeve, just to keep people like me from trying to figure out its secrets. Some albums I couldn't even pick up, I'd look at the covers from a distance. David Bowie's *Diamond Dogs* gave me nightmares. And *Houses of the Holy* too. The dead girl on the cover of Roxy Music, *Goat's Head Soup*. I think the first real album I bought was Carly Simon *Playing Possum* and I only bought that because I heard she shop-lifited the little slip she was wearing and I thought that was so cool. Maybe I just wanted to be them. Joni Mitchell on *Hejira*. Patti Smith on *Horses*. Who didn't want to be Patti Smith on *Horses*? But that was Vic, she owned the Patti Smith thing. I could only aspire to the girl on the cover of *Candy-O* by The Cars. It was so illicit. So dangerous. It started my life. And it started in record stores, and moved to the basement, me lying on the floor watching dust in the sunlight with "Gloria" on those big vinyl headphones.

And then bar rooms and clubs and vans with orange carpeting and motels and it was the road the road the road and how many studios and the road and there goes my life, in the trees blurred through the rain on the bus window, spread out like empty fields from the plane, in the bottles and bottles and bottles and bottles. Then bags to stop the blackouts, nickels then dimes then eightballs. And bottles and bottles and bags and bottles and the road and the airports. And all of it scored, every day a new liner note. And it all started here. In these little records. This was my life. This was what I thought was life. Then it all stopped working. The music went away and the costume changed and I learned a new language and eveything just became art direction and vibrations in the grooves of little black discs.

KAT takes a moment.

I could live in my art but never in my life.

KAT is overwhelmed. The KID approaches KAT and puts her hand on KAT's shoulder. Suddenly the KID is full of comfort and kindness.

KID: It's all just made up anyway. We all make up our own life.

KAT looks at the KID.

It's time.

The KID leaves the room. KAT follows.

48 INT. HIGH SCHOOL HALLWAY - NIGHT

KAT follows the KID down the hallway. Things look different than they did before. Brighter, like another place, another time. KAT looks ahead of her and the KID has disappeared around a corner. KAT follows. The hallways are empty of people.

49 INT. HIGH SCHOOL STAGE - NIGHT

As KAT enters the auditorium it is empty. KAT looks up and sees that the KID is on the stage in a spot of light. She starts a in a version of Siouxsie and the Banshees "Hongkong Garden." Behind her we see a drummer behind a drum kit which has "The Shutups" roughly stencilled on it. The KID is YOUNG KAT. Another young woman enters YOUNG KAT's spotlight and joins her in the song. This is YOUNG VIC.

KAT watches her younger self, her best friend, her past, as it plays out before her. It bothers her that it's so familiar. She turns and walks out an exit. When the door closes behind the sound of the real party returns.

50 EXT. HIGH SCHOOL GIRL'S ROOM - NIGHT

VIC and BEEBEE sit on the sinks in the girls' room. They have been having a heavy talk. BEEBEE holds her hand.

BEEBEE: It's all gone now. All that shit. All those fucking sunrises with no sleep, all those emergency rooms, all those bad men, those bad bad men. And now it's afterward you know?

VIC: Yeah yeah.

BEEBEE: And afterward it's just family. That's all we've fucking got. All these losers and drug addicts and bankrupt souls. But it's family.

VIC: Yeah.

BEEBEE: And that's me for you. Family.

VIC: And Kat too.

BEEBEE: I don't know, I think she sets you off.

VIC: Maybe I set her off.

BEEBEE: You good though? You clean?

VIC: Yeah.

BEEBEE: What about Kat?

VIC: Yeah. I mean according to her yeah.

BEEBEE: It's easier for us junkies. We've got the threat of jail. The drunks, all they've got to worry about is blackouts and cirrhosis.

VIC: Yeah well, that's something to worry about.

BEEBEE: Let me take you home.

VIC: Kat's got a cab waiting.

BEEBEE: I mean let me take you home with me.

VIC: Oh…

BEEBEE: You're so fucking beautiful.

BEEBEE kisses VIC on the lips. The kiss lingers. VIC moves away.

VIC: This feels a bit incest-y for "family".

BEEBEE: Yeah yeah. If you change your mind…

VIC: Yeah yeah, you're the first in line.

BEEBEE: I guess it makes sense you'd go home with the cash machine since she paid for the whole night.

VIC: Who?

BEEBEE: Kat. Apparently she put up the dinero for the shindig.

VIC: I think I'd know that if she did.

BEEBEE: I guess my sources aren't all that reliable.

VIC: Later.

VIC moves away to leave. BEEBEE calls after her.

BEEBEE: If you just want a lift I've got a car. A Hybrid. I'm saving the planet. Fucking pinch me.

VIC: Right on.

BEEBEE: It's the family afterward.

VIC: Yeah.

VIC is gone. In a stall a toilet flushes. The door of the stall opens and BUCKY emerges looking ill.

BUCKY: Nothing's fun.

BEEBEE: Oh baby, I know. I know baby.

51 INT. HIGH SCHOOL FOYER - NIGHT

VIC wanders through the crowd looking for KAT.

52 EXT. HIGH SCHOOL - NIGHT 52

VIC walks out of the high school and looks for KAT. She sees her standing near the cab talking with the CABBIE who leans on the hood. VIC approaches them. She comes upon KAT suddenly.

VIC: Hey.

KAT turns surprised.

You want to head out?

Not being able to hold it in any longer KAT exhales a lungful of smoke. She looks at the joint she holds in her fingers and guiltily hands it to the CABBIE. VIC looks at KAT with disgust and turns and walks away. KAT follows after her.

KAT: Hey, hey what's up, hold on.

VIC: Yeah you're clean and sober.

CABBIE: *(Calling after KAT.)* Where's the other half of the hundred?.

KAT rushes back and gives him the other half of the hundred dollar bill then moves to catch up to VIC who heads back toward the high school.

KAT: It's no big deal. It wasn't mine, it was his.

VIC: I wonder if his company knows he gets high and drives? I should give them a call.

KAT: When did you start snitching to employers?

VIC: You're still exactly the same. Say one thing and do another.

KAT: I never said I wasn't smoking pot. Pot's not my problem.

VIC: It's all a problem.

KAT: For you maybe. Hey lighten up.Where are you going?

VIC: Beebee's going to take me home.

KAT: Wait.

53 INT. HIGH SCHOOL HALLWAY - NIGHT

KAT follows VIC as she walks quickly through the crowded hallway of the high school.

KAT: We'll take the cab.

VIC: I'm not driving with someone high.

KAT: Well call another cab. I'll call a cab.

VIC: I'd rather go with Beebee.

KAT: I'm not living up to your expectations and you want to write me off?

VIC: It's not about my expectations.

KAT: I never tried to sell you on my sainthood.

VIC: Yeah yeah, "sell". That's all you've ever done. Fucking lunchboxes and prostitution.

KAT: What are you talking about?

VIC: I'm not talking to you when you're high.

KAT: I had two hits. It's crappy shit. I'm not even high. I fucked up.

VIC: So now you're apologizing?

KAT: I'm not apologizing.

VIC: Then get the fuck away from me.

KAT: Wait.

VIC stops and turns to KAT.

VIC: I don't want to play this game anymore and I don't want people in my life who play the game.

KAT: What game? It's all a fucking game.

VIC: "What game? It's all a game." That's you all over, you ask the question and answer it in the same breath.

KAT: You think it's not? Wake up sister. Just because you've grown fucking wings doesn't mean the world's turned into heaven.

VIC: Fuck you.

VIC storms off and up a staircase. KAT calls after her.

KAT: Oh good one. You really got me. Nice comeback.

I'll see you after school. Don't forget to do your biology homework. Hey. Hey. Don't walk away from me. Shit.

KAT follows after VIC.

54 INT. HIGH SCHOOL HALLWAY - NIGHT

VIC has gotten well ahead of KAT as she makes her way up an empty hallway of the high school.

KAT: Wait.

VIC: Just leave me alone OK?

KAT: I want to know what your problem is.

VIC: Right now you're my fucking problem.

KAT: Why are you acting like such a fucking maniac?

VIC: I'm working on my shit OK.

KAT: And I'm not?

VIC: Your way. You're working your way. You don't make the rules.

KAT: And you do?

VIC: No. We don't. You know the rules.

VIC can't find the green room. She turns and heads down a flight of stairs.

KAT: Wait. Fucking wait.

55 INT. MULTI-PURPOSE ROOM - NIGHT

VIC pushes through a door into a multi-purpose room with wrestling mats on the floor. KAT follows behind her.

KAT: Wait.

VIC stops and faces KAT.

VIC: If you want to live in a world of bullshit that's fine, at least believe in it. At least believe in something.

KAT: I want to. I do.

VIC stops and faces KAT.

VIC: You put this whole thing together didn't you.

KAT: I… No.

VIC: Don't you think you should have told me that?

KAT: I did some consulting.

VIC: What does that mean?

KAT: I threw some money at it that's all.

VIC: You paid for a tribute for yourself?

KAT: It was a benefit.

VIC: For your ego.

KAT: I just wanted to see you.

VIC: Why?

KAT: I don't know what I need. You say you have what you need. I don't know what that is for me. Nothing is enough. Nothing has ever been enough. I want… I need… You know me, you're the one person who knows me. I do everything I'm supposed to do but… There are all these promises but they aren't coming true. I need you to help me.

VIC: Help you? Fuck.

KAT: Do you have any fucking idea how hard this is for me? Every fucking day? Being sober?

VIC: You and your wine coolers and your cranberry martinis.

KAT: You think I don't want to get high too?

VIC: You just did. Congratulations.

VIC turns and walks away. KAT runs at VIC and tackles her, they roll into the wrestling mats. They struggle for a few moments rolling and pinning one another back and forth, it's a fight yet no one is throwing any punches, it's the way 14-year-old girls might fight. At one point KAT has VIC pinned and VIC breaks free, KAT moves to grab VIC's shoulder and accidentally hits VIC in the mouth.

Ow!

KAT immediately releases VIC.

KAT: Oh my God I'm sorry.

VIC: I'm bleeding.

KAT: I'm sorry I was just trying to—

VIC: Trying to what? You fucking attacked me.

KAT: Just talk to me that's all.

VIC: I'm fucking bleeding.

KAT: Let me see.

KAT looks at VIC's lip.

VIC: OW!

KAT: It's not bleeding.

VIC: Yes it is. *(Touching her lip and showing KAT her finger.)* What's that!

KAT: It's parsley.

VIC: *(Notices that it is.)* Oh. Well it's going to swell up that's for sure, you fucking hit me.

KAT: Just talk to me.

VIC: If you're going to fuck yourself up I don't want to be around to watch it.

KAT: I had two puffs. I got overwhelmed, OK. I've got a lot on my mind.

VIC: Well I've got a lot on my fucking mind too alright. I might be fucking dying.

KAT: What?

VIC: I have to have a fucking liver biopsy that's what.

KAT: You had one or you're having one?

VIC: They saw something.

KAT: You had one or you're having one?

VIC: I'm having one.

KAT: I've had two, it's no big deal. They're always seeing things on my liver.

VIC: You think your liver's in worse shape than mine?

KAT: I know it is.

VIC: My liver's like a sponge.

KAT: It's supposed to be like a sponge. Mine's like a stone.

VIC: I don't think so.

KAT: Don't tell me about my liver.

VIC: Yeah well don't tell me about mine, I know my own liver.

KAT: If you did they wouldn't need to do a biopsy.

VIC: Fuck you.

KAT: Fuck you.

A moment.

Everybody's dying.

VIC: I don't care about the destination I'm more concerned about the velocity.

KAT: Let me see your eyes.

VIC: Why?

KAT: Iridology. I see the best iridologist in L.A.

VIC opens her eyes to KAT.

Uh huh. OK. Uh huh.

VIC: What?

KAT: Move your head a bit. Look up into that light.

VIC does so.

OK. Uh huh.

VIC: What?

KAT: Too much sugar. You eat a lot of sugar?

VIC: I'm trying to cut down.

KAT: And salt. Salt's the real problem. You eat a lot of salt.

VIC: I like salty.

KAT: You've got to cut out the salt. Salt binds the toxins and you can't sweat them out. That's what's happening with your liver. No more salt. Do you read the labels?

VIC: What labels?

KAT: Food labels. There's salt in everything. Do you read the labels?

VIC: The print's too small.

KAT: Wear your glasses when you go to the store. Read the labels. No salt.

VIC: There's something on my liver.

KAT: It's the salt. It is.

VIC: OK. It's the salt.

KAT: It is.

VIC: OK.

VIC gets up.

Let's get the fuck out of here.

KAT moves to get up. Her shoulder pinches. She winces.

What?

KAT: My shoulder goes out sometimes.

VIC: That's not my fault.

KAT: I'm not saying it is.

VIC: You're the one who attacked me.

KAT: Fine fine.

VIC: My lip's killing me.

KAT walks away toward and exit door at the back of the room.

KAT: Come on.

VIC gets up.

VIC: You sure it's not bleeding?

KAT: It's not bleeding.

VIC follows KAT toward the door. KAT's knee goes out.

VIC: What's wrong with your leg?

KAT: It's my knee. From running. I might have to stop running.

VIC: Well you shouldn't be attacking people.

KAT: Yeah yeah.

VIC: Here give me your arm.

Is it your shoulder or your collarbone?

We hear them as they continue to talk, disappearing from view.

KAT: My shoulder.

VIC: Are you sure?

KAT: It's my rotator cuff.

VIC: *(O.S.)* Because you broke your collar bone that time in Cuba when you fell off the moped, it could be-

KAT: *(O.S.)* It's my rotator cuff.

VIC: *(O.S.)* Is that the thing they scrape?

KAT: *(O.S.)* Yeah. They want to do my knee too.

VIC: *(O.S.)* My knees are shit. We're falling apart.

KAT: *(O.S.)* No I think this is just what human ends up feeling like.

Slowly SICK VIC rises up looking down the barrel of the camera. She sticks out her tongue and gives devil fingers. She drops the pose and looks at us.

SICK VIC: Ah fuck y'all. This party sucks.

SICK VIC heads back to the party.

56 INT. CAB - JUST BEFORE DAWN

VIC and KAT sit in the back of a cab heading back downtown.They are quiet, chill. KAT is looking out the window.

KAT: Our hell is a good life.

VIC: Yeah.

KAT holds up her hand for a high five. VIC reaches up and gently puts her hand against KAT's. VIC links her fingers with KAT's. They ride along like this, not looking at one another, not speaking, holding hands.

57 EXT. DOWNTOWN STREET - JUST BEFORE DAWN

KAT and VIC small in the distance, walk along a deserted downtown street. We hear their conversation.

KAT: We sang the song.

VIC: Our hit.

KAT: Our greatest hit.

VIC: We should release it as an EP.

KAT: A single.

VIC: A 45.

VIC begins to sing "Standing Alongside Gone". It is gentle, sweet, almost a lullaby. KAT begins to sing with her. Two girls, out all night, going home, they will always remember this.

58 EXT. DOWNTOWN PARK - JUST BEFORE DAWN

VIC and KAT have found their way back downtown and sit in a city park. The sit on a bench watching something.

Nearby under a tree three ASIAN SENIOR CITIZENS do a graceful and slow T'ai Chi routine.

KAT: Now there's a vision for you.

VIC: *(Re: T'ai Chi.)* I always wanted to do that.

KAT: You always used to say you wanted to snowshoe.

VIC: Yeah yeah, and I did.

KAT: How was it?

VIC: Brutal. Cold.

KAT: What did you expect?

VIC: Elation?

KAT: That's setting the bar a bit high.

After a moment.

VIC: But I did though. Feel something like that. Elation. But it was afterward, sitting at the fire thinking about having snowshoed.That's the thing isn't it. It's not the doing it that feels good, it's the having done it.

KAT: It's the surviving it.

A moment.

VIC: What if the sun doesn't come up?

KAT: The sun will come up.

VIC: What if the Mayans were right? The calendar stops and it all just ends?

KAT: Wasn't that already supposed to have happened?

VIC: And the earth explodes into four flaming orbs.

KAT: A flaming orb?

VIC: According to the Mayans four flaming orbs.

KAT: Nice.

VIC: Just ends. Everything reduced to balls of ash and melted plastic hurtling through space.

A moment.

What difference does it all make then? All the music, the gigs, the deals, the art, the beauty, the men, the Jager, the pregnancy tests, the bad biopsies... Or maybe that's it. There is no everything, it's just me and my everything. My calendar. My ending.

A moment.

KAT: A flaming orb.

VIC: Four flaming orbs.

KAT: Which would be like four suns. Right? And since

the sun starts the Universe, there you go, you've got four whole new Universes.

VIC: Four Universes of fuck up.

KAT: And wonder. See that's what people want, not sex, not more stuff, what people want is wonder. That's what a new world is all about. Wonder. What more can you ask for? Four Universes of fuck up and wonder. That's progress.

VIC: That's something.

KAT: It's cold.

VIC: Do you want your sweater?

KAT: Nah, keep it.

They sit silently a moment.

This is nice.

VIC: Yeah. It's nice.

VIC and KAT sit on the bench watching as the sun slowly rises, the buildings of the city glow. It is stunning, perfect light.

KAT: *(Amazed.)* God…

VIC: *(Staring into the light.)* Yeah.

KAT looks at VIC.

The End.